Young Marilyn

'I went to work at Radioplane Company. They had some photographers there taking moving pictures for army training. An army corporal with the 1st Motion Picture Unit told me he would be interested in getting some still shots of me, so I posed for him. He said that I should go into modelling.'

NORMA JEANE, 1945

'I suppose you're with *that business*? I'm a Christian Scientist. I work for the church. I don't work with the moving-picture industry. I don't even have radio or television, see? My work is diametrically opposite to that, you know, to what she was doing in the moving picture industry.'

It was 7 April 1972, and I was listening to Gladys Eley's reminiscences, while my two small sons, Dean and Michael, were playing nearby, drawing. I felt awestruck at fate allowing me to be there, talking, with the mother of a movie legend. There was no mistaking Gladys Eley as other than the mother of Marilyn Monroe.

A gentle, smiling woman, then in her seventies, her eyes were identical to her daughter's, and with her girlish charm and luminous skin, her laugh, it was as if I were sitting there once again with Marilyn.

Reaching back across the years, Gladys recalled: 'I never wanted her to be in that business. Of course, I never told her one way or the other; I never told her a word.'

Marilyn Monroe is possibly the subject of more Hollywood-inspired folklore than any other cinematic legend. And her myth has been added to by many, from actor Ben Lyon, the man who first called her Marilyn Monroe, to the American writer, Norman Mailer. Even Marilyn herself helped it along from time to time over the years.

Given the infinite number of conflicting versions of Marilyn Monroe's early years in Hollywood — her starlet days — it becomes hard to sort out fact from fiction. And so the purpose of this narrative, which relies specifically on documented yet rarely published facts of the early days of her career from 1945 to 1953, is to get at the truth about those years.

Any intimate exploration of Marilyn Monroe's life during these years usually includes accounts, always varying ones that depend on the biographer, of her relationships, both professional and personal, with a variety of people in the Hollywood milieu at that time. Much of this has been well documented in each and every one of the Monroe biographies, from Maurice Zolotow's to Anthony Summers'. Therefore, in the interests of not repeating an oft-told tale, they will be omitted from this narrative. And, while I knew Marilyn personally from 1954 until her death in 1962, I have no desire to interpret or misinterpret her relationships with others. As to her starlet past, she herself recalled in 1955: 'I modelled, and then I was under contract to Fox. After some magazine covers appeared they signed me.' It was that simple, but not that easy.

Young Marilyn

BECOMING THE LEGEND

James Haspiel

HYPERION

NEW YORK

This work is enthusiastically dedicated with
much love to my brilliant younger son, the clever, always witty
showstopper known as Mike

MICHAEL DAVID HASPIEL

First published in Great Britain in 1994 by Smith Gryphon Ltd, London

Copyright © 1994 by James Haspiel

ISBN 0-7868-6077-4

FIRST AMERICAN EDITION
10 9 8 7 6 5 4 3 2 1

Designed by Hammond Hammond
Printed in Italy by New Interlitho SpA

PAGE 1
This 1945 portrait of model Norma Jeane was to become the
cover of Salute magazine in August 1946.

PAGE 2
Young Marilyn sits for an early portrait during her first days at
the 20th Century-Fox studio, c. 1946.

PAGE 4
Skiing on sand, the newly named Marilyn Monroe poses for
publicity fodder, c. 1946–7.

PAGE 6
Marilyn poses poolside in Hollywood c. 1948.

PAGES 8 & 9
Taken c. 1947, this yellow-bikinied image of Marilyn was later
to become a postcard in the 1950s – and again in the 1960s –
and yet again in the 1990s.

CONTENTS

CHAPTER ONE

Becoming Marilyn

On the morning of 2 August 1945, 19-year-old Norma Jeane Dougherty left her West Los Angeles apartment at 11348 Nebraska Avenue. As she stepped out into the warm California sunshine and made her way to the Blue Book Model Agency, she was embarking unwittingly on a journey that would ultimately make movie history. It was one that would not end 17 years later with her untimely death but continue to be woven into cinematic folklore for ever.

That August day her future was far from certain. At the agency she filled out a registration card, complete with her phone number, Arizona 3-2487, and went back home. She was later to make her first professional appearance in front of a movie camera through Blue Book, as she smiled into the camera lens over a screen credit that announced her by her then married name: Norma Jean Dougherty. Jean was slightly misspelt – without the 'e' that appears at the end of it on her birth certificate, the Jeane that she used throughout her life in her signature.

This was, nevertheless, Marilyn Monroe's first film test. Little did she or anyone else suspect how her image would be destined to be imprisoned on untold reels of celluloid throughout almost the next two decades, to the delight and enjoyment of millions of movie-goers.

Signed on with Blue Book, Norma Jeane worked hard at her career. By the following year, she had appeared on her first magazine cover – holding a lamb on the 26 April issue of *Family Circle* – and

Overlooking Malibu, California, Norma Jeane Dougherty poses for her first cheesecake pin-up, *c.* 1945.

was popular enough to go on later that year to grace four magazine covers in one month. It was through these cover-girl appearances that she caught the ever watchful eye of the Hollywood film industry, always on the look-out for beautiful young girls – potential starlets.

That summer of 1946, 17 July to be exact, Norma Jeane walked through the gates of the fabled 20th Century-Fox film studios for the first time. It was her introduction to the burgeoning world of American cinema, and on the set of the Betty Grable film, *Mother Wore Tights*, then in preproduction, cameraman Leon Shamroy was waiting for her. His camera loaded with a 100-ft roll of silent colour film stock, he was ready to make her screen test for Fox.

The filming took no time at all, but the weeks that followed must have felt like an eternity to the aspiring starlet. The end of July came with no word from Fox, while she worked as a cover girl for *Laff*, on which she was identified as Jean Norman, as well as for *Pageant*, *Salute* and *US Camera* magazines. August arrived and passed slowly into its final week before, on 26 August 1946, Fox finally signed her to a beginner's contract.

It was Marilyn's first break in Hollywood, and inexorably the wheels that powered the change in her life began to be set in motion. Initially around her name. She had entered the studio as Norma Jeane Dougherty but within weeks was given the more exotic title of Marilyn Monroe. This was Ben Lyon's doing – the very actor who had starred opposite Jean Harlow in *Hell's Angels* – who was at that time the head of Fox's casting department. And then within her personal life: just five weeks after signing her contract she would divorce her husband, Jim Dougherty.

On 5 September 1946, *Variety* carried the mention of 'Jane Ball and Norma Jeane Dougherty signed to new contracts at 20th-Fox.' Now the bona fide property of a major motion-picture studio, as with all new contract players with no prior experience in front of movie cameras, Norma Jeane, about to be reborn as Marilyn, was quickly pressed into service as an extra in a number of Fox's current pro-

'Starlet-Caddy' Marilyn at a Cheviot Hills Golf Benefit, in the Los Angeles of July 1947.

Marilyn as photographed
on a California beach
c. 1947.

Before there was a young
Marilyn, there was the
young Norma Jeane, who
wrote this vintage
postcard from a vacation
in Chicago in October 1944.

HOLLYWOOD
merry·go·round

Three Starlets From "Mother Wore Tights" Get An Off-Season Sun Tan

Sun lamps will do the trick, when even California weather gets a bit chilly for outdoor tanning. Donna Hamilton smooths more lotion on Marilyn Monroe's back.

Bob Landry

OLIVIA de HAVILLAND received a floral good-luck wish when she began work on *The Snake Pit*. It was a huge bouquet from husband Marcus Goodrich. She put the flowers before her dressing-room mirror. "I'd much rather look at them than myself," she said. Incidentally, Olivia tells us that she wants to do a Broadway play, just for variety.

AL JOLSON, say fans all over the country, got too much credit for *The Jolson Story* success; Larry Parks, not enough. So much publicity was turned on Al that Larry was almost lost in the shuffle. But the fans love Larry—you can take our word for it. We read the mail! Turn to page 25 and follow Larry to Mexico.

Donna tunes in soft music for Marilyn and their hostess, Marjorie Holliday (right), also from 20th Century-Fox.

ORSON WELLES, recently master-mind on *The Lady From Shanghai*, tells this story on himself: He opened a play one night during a blizzard that tied up traffic; and only eight people showed up. When Orson made his curtain speech, he said, "I am Orson Welles—writer, director, actor, raconteur, painter, sculptor, magician. Isn't it a pity that there are so many of me—and so few of you?"

Fair-skinned Marilyn has to make her sun-lamp sessions short. She is in Betty Grable's *Mother Wore Tights*.

10

CONTINUED ON PAGE 12

ductions. It was then that various of their publicity releases credit Monroe with appearances in *Mother Wore Tights, The Shocking Miss Pilgrim, You Were Meant for Me, The Challenge* and *Green Grass of Wyoming.*

The Shocking Miss Pilgrim was a 1947 release about women's equal rights to employment in 1847, prior to the invention of the telephone, in which the *Australian Film Guide*'s June 1966 issue lists Monroe as an extra. Joel Greenberg, in his summer 1974 *Focus on Film* article on the director Walter Lang notes: 'In George Seaton's *The Shocking Miss Pilgrim* Marilyn Monroe had a bit part as a switchboard operator.' And another publicity source firmly places Marilyn as an extra on the film.

Closer scrutiny of the film's production charts in contemporary issues of the *Hollywood Reporter* reveals, however, that *Pilgrim* completed filming in February 1946, six months before Fox first signed Monroe. Yet this contradiction may just be resolved by the possibility of a montage of general scenes, such as women at work in the future, including the switchboard operator sequence, being filmed later and then cut from the film before its release in 1947.

Mother Wore Tights is equally hazy. Fredda Dudley, writing in the September 1950 issue of *Photoplay* magazine, claimed that Marilyn Monroe had 'worked, without lines, in *Mother Wore Tights* with Betty Grable'. While this is possible, it may be that Monroe's credit came simply from the fact that she had filmed her silent screen test on the *Mother Wore Tights* set.

There again, a fading page from an old movie magazine carries the headline: HOLLYWOOD MERRY-GO-ROUND: THREE STARLETS FROM *MOTHER WORE TIGHTS* GET AN OFF-SEASON SUN TAN. Marilyn Monroe, Donna Hamilton and Marjorie Holliday are featured in a set of photographs, one captioned: 'Fair-skinned Marilyn has to make her sun-lamp sessions short. She is in Betty Grable's *Mother Wore Tights.*'

Both *Mother Wore Tights* and *Green Grass of Wyoming* were filmed during Monroe's first tenure at Fox, so it is probable that she

This fading page from an old movie magazine announces Marilyn Monroe's appearance in the 20th Century-Fox film, *Mother Wore Tights.*

Caught short (braless, that
is) in an early calendar pose.

Peekaboo! Marilyn
displays a little more than
would be allowed in
magazines of the 1940s,
in this calendar-bound
pin-up.

appeared as an extra in them. However, Fredda Dudley is not always so accurate. When she reported that 'Her next picture was *The Big Wheel*, in which she had three lines,' it appears that she was confusing this film, starring Mickey Rooney, with another, *The Fireball*, in which, in fact, Marilyn shared a few scenes with Rooney.

Film titles often go through several incarnations before release, and Dudley's – and others' – confusion may be better understood by knowing that *The Challenge* was in fact the original working title of *The Fireball*.

But the 1948 release, *The Challenge*, is credited to Marilyn Monroe in a comprehensive listing of her films published in Europe and stars Tom Conway as Bulldog Drummond. It has all but disappeared. Nevertheless it should not be mistaken for the number of other movies that share the same title, in particular a 1960 British import, retitled *It Takes a Thief* for its American release and starring Marilyn Monroe's celluloid shadow, Jayne Mansfield.

It may never be known for sure whether or not Marilyn Monroe appears in any of the movies mentioned so far. But, *You Were Meant for Me*, filming of which commenced in September 1947 after Monroe's contractual release from Fox, is cited without its title by Monroe herself in an interview: 'You might have seen a 67-second close-up of my back during one of the dance numbers.'

It appears she may well have returned to Fox's sound stages on extra duty, maybe from Central Casting, which could also better explain her earlier credit for *The Shocking Miss Pilgrim*. In fact there is a scene in *You Were Meant for Me* at a college dance – one of many – in which the camera pans a crowded dance floor, capturing among the many bobbing heads a fleeting, Marilynesque face. It's possible to spot her by freeze framing the scene. And this sighting is also supported by the June 1966 edition of the *Australian Film Guide* that places Monroe as an extra in the picture.

Whatever columinist Sheilah Graham may have to say about Monroe's role in *You Were Meant for Me* as having 'expired on the

An already published image from this moment is sometimes credited as one of Marilyn filming her first Fox screen test, but this never before seen image is more likely the fledgling actress on the set of *You Were Meant for Me*, in which she worked as an extra in 1947.

cutting room floor', and however many biographers cite her screen career as starting some time later, one fact is indisputable. Monroe could not have reported to work at a major motion-picture studio for nearly a year of her contract without appearing in front of at least some of their cameras.

Monroe's own vagueness about her early film career, which doesn't help to establish its facts, was explained succinctly by two-time Academy Award winner Shelley Winters. Winters' memories of Marilyn seemed clear as she recalled for me the time in the late 1940s when they both attended a big Hollywood première, the two of them unknown actresses huddled together in the bleachers watching the movie stars arrive at the first-night screening: 'We were two happy kids having fun.'

However, Winters also talks of the fear new contract players can experience during their first months at a motion-picture studio. She described how she herself was moved from film to film, sometimes working as an extra on more than one production in a single day, and how she was not able to recall the title of many of the films in which she'd appeared before reaching her first professional recognition.

Such acknowledgement must have felt far from her grasp when, for legal reasons, Marilyn Monroe/Norma Jeane Dougherty double-signed her six-months renewal contract with 20th Century-Fox on 10 February 1947. She couldn't have known then, nor would her optimism have allowed, that genuine movie stardom would continue to elude her for some years to come.

In her candy-stripe bikini, young Marilyn shows off her flawless alabaster skin in the California sunshine of 1947.

.   .   .

The 16 February edition of the *Chicago Sun's Parade* magazine saw Monroe smiling brightly on its cover. And the smile was not misplaced as finally, in the spring of 1947, Marilyn was assigned a speaking part, albeit a very small one, in a Fox film to be called *Scudda Hoo! Scudda Hay!* Also released under its alternate title of *Summer Lightning*, it was shot in Technicolor and released in movie theatres the following year.

In a curious twist of fate, our legendary sex symbol was to utter her first movie dialogue not in a seductive setting dressed in a glamorous evening gown but instead on the steps of a church wearing a simple peasant costume. Very few movie-goers would suspect this unexplored side of the Monroe character, except for the exquisite abbey scenes in *The Prince and the Showgirl* a full decade later, might be as close to the real girl as any of the subsequent scriptwriters' wildest bedroom fantasies.

We fade into *Scudda Hoo! Scudda Hay!* and find the film's star, June Haver, and a moppet-sized Natalie Wood engaged in conversation outside a church, following the Sunday service. Parishioners are coming out of the doors of the church behind them, among them a young blonde dressed in a blue and white pinafore. As the girl walks across the screen from right to left, she turns to Haver and says, 'Hi, Rad,' to which Haver responds, 'Hi, Betty.' Betty is, of course, Marilyn Monroe.

Monroe's appearance consumes little more than seconds of screen time. Moments later there is another scene, this time by a lake. Here in the background we see two girls in a boat, rowing, their backs to the camera as they slowly fade from view. One of the girls, the blonde, offers the audience another sighting of Marilyn.

Later, when Monroe had become a star, her Fox publicity releases started the myth that the *Scudda Hoo! Scudda Hay!* scene, in which she had greeted June Haver, publicized as her 'screen debut', had 'landed on the cutting room floor'. Not so. Despite the fact that every Monroe biography has repeated this tale, and Marilyn herself even volunteered it as fact as late as 8 April 1955 during a live appearance on Edward R. Murrow's Person To Person television show, the truth remains that the scene was not cut. Movie buffs and television addicts can still view this tiny piece of cinema history wherever *Scudda Hoo! Scudda Hay!* shows up.

Soon after her two scenes in *Scudda Hoo! Scudda Hay!* were completed, Monroe worked in a second speaking part at Fox, playing a waitress in *Dangerous Years*. This time, in addition to having several lines of dialogue, Marilyn was given her first big screen close-

The yet unknown Marilyn Monroe is the centrepiece in this rare photo of the cast and crew of 20th Century-Fox's *Scudda Hoo! Scudda Hay!*, taken on 26 April 1947, the day of her movie debut.

up, a progression not to be underrated in the establishment of an actor's image with the movie-going public.

However, this may have appeared as less than a triumph at the time. When Monroe filmed this small role in August 1947, it was just days before she was dropped by 20th Century-Fox. It was to be her first experience of the studio's high turnover of its contract players at option time.

The girl who decorated the cover of France's *Cine Monde* magazine for her momentary appearance in *Scudda Hoo! Scudda Hay!* made no secret of the Fox interlude: 'They dropped me after a year,' going on to confirm the myth of the lost debut scene: 'I didn't have an opportunity to do anything, actually, during the year that I was there . . . except for one part in *Scudda Hoo! Scudda Hay!*, and I was cut out of it, so you can't exactly call that a chance to do anything.' She made no mention of *Dangerous Years*.

Following her time at Fox, Monroe found herself playing that most awkward of Hollywood roles: the dropped, freelance starlet model. She nevertheless persisted in her efforts to make it as an actress. Needing to stay in the limelight, she continued to pose for pin-up magazines and appeared regularly on the covers of *Glamorous Models*, *Laff* and *Personal Romance*, among others. She also took part in publicity stunts, such as appearing as a Starlet Caddy at a Cheviot Hills Golf Benefit in Los Angeles, and around this period she was the face that hawked Nesbitt's California Orange Drink.

Glamour Preferred might have been Marilyn Monroe's byline, and it was her appearance as second female lead in this revival of Florence Ryerson and Colin Clement's 1940 Broadway stage play that got her working as an actress again. She had answered a casting-call ad that appeared in the *Los Angeles Times* of 21 September 1947 and got the part of a movie star, a siren of the silver screen, in a satirical comedy on life in Hollywood. Her tenacity had paid off. Ironically, it was at the Bliss-Hayden Miniature Theatre in Beverly Hills that Monroe got to act out her own dreams and aspirations.

A provocative Marilyn in Hollywood at the age of 22.

The theatre, which no longer exists, was then located at 254 South Robertson Boulevard. It was started by actor Harry Hayden, a veteran of stage, screen and television, and his actress wife, Lela Bliss. Established in the 1930s, the Bliss-Hayden Theatre doubled as a showcase for both cinema and the stage. It was a useful forum for aspiring movie stars, who hoped to be spotted by the frequent studio talent scouts in the audience.

This was not an idle fantasy. At various times, members of the Bliss-Hayden Players, offspring of Lela and Harry Hayden's School of Theatre, included Jon Hall, Veronica Lake, Robert Hutton, Doris Day, Craig Stevens and Debbie Reynolds.

The cast for a Bliss-Hayden production would be assembled from their students, though sometimes an outsider was brought in for a particular role. By design, each role would be played on consecutive nights by different student-actors, each scheduled to appear according to strict rotation. This way the actors could watch each other, comparing and learning from their own and each other's performance.

Harry Hayden worked as drama coach, tapping his own extensive acting experience. When he died in 1955 at the age of 71, the 25 July edition of the *New York Herald Tribune* noted his productivity at the Bliss-Hayden Miniature Theatre with a mention of how, 'such screen stars as Marilyn Monroe . . . studied there.'

There is, however, not much to go on about Monroe's appearance in *Glamour Preferred*. What is known, though, is that it opened on the evening of 12 October 1947, scheduled for a run of three weeks, thus closing on 2 November. Neither the *Los Angeles Times* nor the *Citizen News* carried a review of the play, possibly because an earlier production had opened in the Los Angeles area the previous June, and the play itself may have been reviewed then.

Whatever the reasons, this lack of press coverage increased the futility of any struggle to pin down the facts about the play as they relate to Marilyn Monroe. Eventually, however, a lead came from the

Above Bill Eythe smiles at out-on-the-town starlet Marilyn Monroe as Bill Callahan looks on at the opening of *Lend an Ear*, at the Las Palmas Theatre in Hollywood, 1948.

Left Marilyn in the make-up department at Columbia Pictures, 1948, being prepared for her first sizeable movie role in *Ladies of the Chorus*.

This never before seen image of a young and glorious Marilyn was captured at the Town House pool, Hollywood, in July 1948.

Los Angeles Public Library, when librarian Evelyn Champagne tracked down Lela Bliss Hayden for me and tape-recorded an interview with her in February 1975, which began with Champagne explaining: 'Mr Haspiel was just so fascinated by the fact that nobody has paid any atention to Marilyn Monroe's stage experience.'

With nearly three decades having passed since she had worked with Monroe. Lela Bliss Hayden could still recall that time: 'She didn't play anywhere else but at our theatre. We had Marilyn for about eight months, when she was, I would say, between 16 and 17. [Monroe was, in fact, 21 at the time of *Glamour Preferred*.]

'I don't remember everything. I think '47 would be about the time to date her stage career, maybe a little earlier. You know, they tried to sell her as a sex symbol; she wasn't a sexy girl, really. I don't mean that she didn't have appeal, but she was a nice little girl. I didn't care as much for her when they worked on her being a sex symbol as I did when she was just a . . . just a lovely girl.'

When asked whether Monroe had appeared in any other of the theatre's productions, Lela had only the vaguest recollection: 'Well, I know she was, but I don't know what they were.' However, her actor son, Don Hayden, had a more definite memory of Monroe's appearance in their production of *Stage Door*, which opened in mid-August 1948 and played through to 12 September.

The Haydens had enjoyed something of a unique reputation in their heyday in Hollywood. Lela mentioned those times: 'We had the theatre from 1934 until about 1952. Harry directed the plays, and I trained the students to speak. Most of them spoke horribly; they would leave their gs off havin' and goin', and you can't have that, you know. [Was this the birth of Monroe's perfect diction?]

'It takes a lot of work to clean a voice up. I still excel in that. I still teach. I have some lovely girls now. They're so smart, you know; I think the young people are smarter today than they were when I was a young girl.'

Lela Bliss Hayden then became more specific again about Marilyn Monroe: 'She could have played anything. We never had any struggle

Sex symbol on ice, Marilyn poses for a pin-up portrait at Columbia Pictures in 1948.

about parts with her, she was always happy to play what you cast her in. And when Mr Billy Grady, the casting director at Metro-Goldwyn-Mayer, saw her, he thought she was a *bet*, and he had her come out to the studio, and she got her first job there. I saw it; she was lovely in it.'

Ignoring MM's earlier film appearances, Lela was speaking about Monroe's part in *The Asphalt Jungle*, filmed in the autumn of 1949. This was a year when Bliss Hayden had other fond memories too. Although Monroe had left the theatre the previous year, she recalled Marilyn visiting them when still in her pre-sex symbol days in 1949: 'The night my son left for Europe, we had a little party over at the house, and why she was just as nice a little lady as you would ever see.'

Marilyn Monroe's brush with theatre was shortlived and uneventful but a necessary staging-post in her acting career. Years later she was to have some fun with her theatrical past. In New York City, 1955, when she was a well-established screen star, she took to the stage again for one night only – this time at the Martin Beck Theatre on Broadway and, of course, anonymously. Her face was by then a household item, so her one-night cameo in a performance of *The Teahouse of the August Moon* required a heavy disguise. Nobody spotted her. She only did it for a lark and even took curtain bows with the chorus-line without being recognized.

· · ·

In Hollywood in 1947, on stage at the Bliss-Hayden Theatre, she would have done almost anything to be acknowledged, but this recognition would have to wait as the closing night of *Glamour Preferred* cast her adrift once again. The last weeks of 1947 slipped into 1948 as in February *Dangerous Years* provided the public with a first glimpse of Monroe on screen. This was followed by *Scudda Hoo! Scudda Hay!*, which was reviewed on 3 March by *Variety*, her name appearing in the cast listings as Rad's girlfriend.

It was proving a fallow time, but the seeds Monroe had sown in her diligent pursuit of an acting career began to sprout again just a few days after that *Variety* listing. On 9 March 1948 she was no longer just Rad's girlfriend in *Scudda Hoo! Scudda Hay!* but suddenly the property of another motion-picture studio: Columbia Pictures had signed her exclusively.

But Marilyn's professional triumph was clouded by personal tragedy. A week after her signing to Columbia, Monroe's 'aunt', Ana Lower, died. Lower was the person whom, in Marilyn's own words, she loved most in the world. On 19 March Ana Lower was buried in an unmarked grave – although a small memorial plaque was placed by the site some years later – in the same cemetery, Westwood Memorial Park, that some 14 years later would be witness to Joe DiMaggio's grief as he stood there at Marilyn's own crypt.

Marilyn Monroe reported back to Columbia Pictures shortly after the burial. In a pattern that was to emerge repeatedly throughout her short life, she was tugged two ways emotionally. She felt grief and loss at Ana Lower's death, but jubilation at her first leading role in a feature film. She had landed her first sizeable movie part, playing a burlesque queen – though in the moral climate of 1948 not one garment was shed – in Columbia's *Ladies of the Chorus*. The film was produced in only 11 days.

The speed of her signing at Columbia, her first major screen role and the personal sadness at Ana Lower's death were all critical moments in Marilyn Monroe's life that spring of 1948. They were followed by a distinct emotional tailing-off into actors' limbo land. During her stay at Columbia Pictures Marilyn made only one other known appearance in a feature film, this time in a part that was of no size or stature whatsoever; in fact her presence in person was not even required.

In *Riders of the Whistling Pines* a rancher serenades a photograph of his friend's deceased wife, which is actually a studio portrait still of Marilyn. And that was almost it. Except for Marilyn's

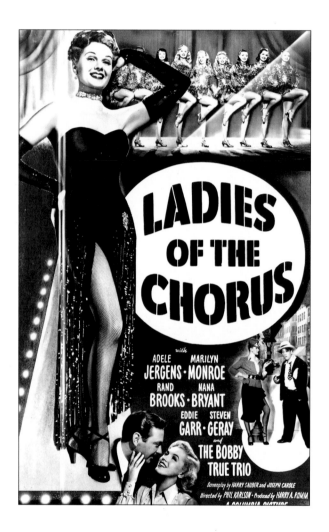

The original poster for the 1948 release of Columbia Pictures' *Ladies of the Chorus*.

Above Marilyn sings 'Every Baby Needs a Da-da-daddy' in *Ladies of the Chorus*. The number turned out to be the highlight of an otherwise forgettable film.

Right Adapting the above image, the 1952 re-issue poster for Columbia's *Ladies of the Chorus* top bills former under-the-title player Marilyn Monroe.

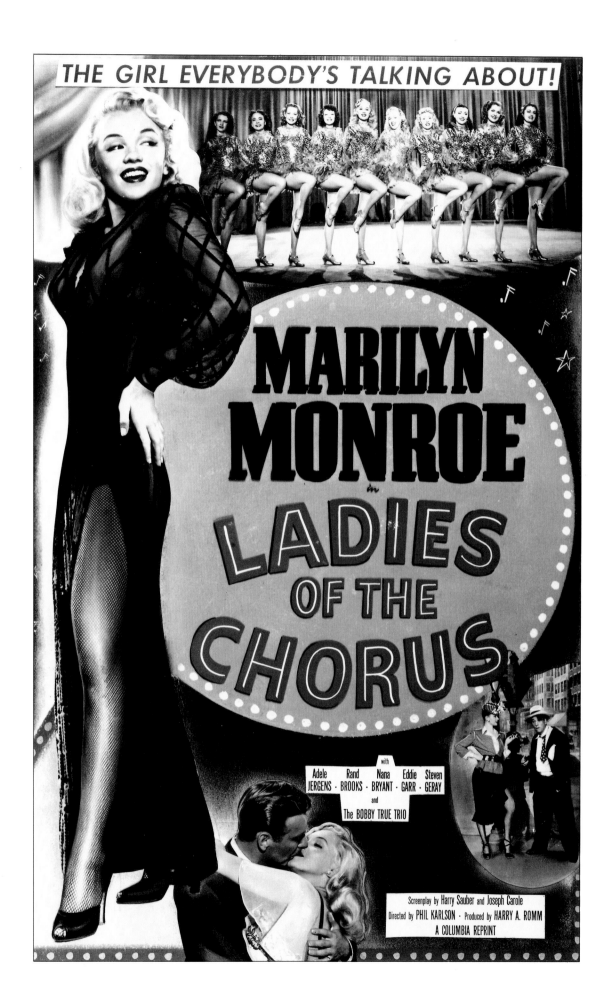

confirmation, on page 63 of her supposed autobiography, *My Story* (1974), where she is quoted from a long-lost manuscript ghosted by Ben Hecht as having done some extra work for Columbia: 'I received several extra girl calls from the studio and worked in a few scenes as background.'

It is curious that with production levels in Hollywood then at a peak – an examination of Columbia's production charts for the period reveals that 28 features were made during Monroe's brief tenure there – Marilyn made no other appearance in any other Columbia film of that time. Other than her own apparent assertion that she had appeared variously as an extra, nothing else has ever been produced to negate the fact that her appearances at Columbia were minimal.

Apart, that is, from failed opportunities. Garson Kanin, in his book *Tracy and Hepburn* (1971), claims that while still at Columbia Pictures, Marilyn Monroe was screen tested for the Billie Dawn role in their film version of *Born Yesterday* – a characterization that later, incidentally, won an Academy Award for Judy Holliday. About Monroe's test Kanin says: 'Those who saw it thought it was excellent. But Harry Cohn, the head of the studio, did not trouble to take the six steps from his desk to his projection room to look at her.'

Later Marilyn would herself lament: 'When you're an obscure bit-player or starlet, nobody cares whether you can act. But when your name is up in lights, it's different.'

Monroe's contract expired on 8 September 1948, and it was not renewed. This some say occurred as a result of her refusal to share an intimate weekend with Harry Cohn. Marilyn Monroe was not deterred. When a friend asked of her, 'If 50 per cent of the experts in Hollywood said you had no talent and should give up, what would you do?', Marilyn responded, 'Look, if 100 per cent told me that, all 100 per cent would be wrong. That's why I'm studying acting and singing. I believe if I can make myself the best actress there is, I have to reach the top.'

In an ironic twist that belongs only to the world of hype and illusion that Hollywood sometimes is, the 1952 re-release of *Ladies of the Chorus* was launched with the name Marilyn Monroe in first billing above the title. And even later in 1952 Columbia was not slow to recognize the current value of their ertswhile reject. In their production of *Okinawa*, a war film, we see a group of restless servicemen invited to watch a clip of Marilyn's singing and dancing routine to 'Every Baby Needs a Da-da-daddy', her musical highspot in *Ladies of the Chorus*. Such are the fickle rewards of fame for both the artist and their backers.

CHAPTER TWO

Start Days

In the autumn of 1948 there were no rich pickings to exploit. Marilyn, released from any contractual obligations to Columbia, had to survive as best she could in the jungle of her chosen profession. Her priorities were first and foremost not to prostitute herself to the world of show business.

The Mayan Theatre is located in downtown Los Angeles. As Monroe says in *The Misfits*, in her role as the Reno divorcee, a character based on her own life: 'I used to dance in places.' Rumour has it that Monroe put the ecdysiast training that she had acquired from the requirements of her part in *Ladies of the Chorus* to some use there in performances to the musical back-up of 'Dream Lover', 'Slow Boat to China', 'Deep Night' and 'It's Magic'.

Her time at the Mayan Theatre, however, would have demanded somewhat more of her than had been asked as the burlesque queen in *Ladies of the Chorus*. Yet, in the tamer world of burlesque of 1948, she would have been spared the indignities of having to expose on stage the more intimate parts of her body, given the legal strictures that existed at that time. Presumably the lure of an admiring audience at Grauman's (now Mann's) Chinese Theatre, Hollywood, was greater and far more inviting to her than any amount of cat calls that might reach her from the men seated beyond the footlights at the Mayan.

Monroe's rumoured time at the Mayan Theatre can not be guaranteed. Whatever truth may surround it, there is one fact that should be aired in connection to it: Dixie Evans.

Evans was a professional striptease artist, a Marilynesque young woman, who appeared in the burlesque houses in and around Los Angeles during the time that Marilyn herself is supposed to have appeared at the Mayan. Indeed the same Ms Evans later exploited her similarity to Marilyn Monroe extensively, in an act that began around

Marilyn Monroe sits for a studio glamour portrait at 20th Century-Fox in 1950.

1952 and ran for more than a decade in burlesque theatres and night-clubs. For those years Dixie Evans was billed as THE MARILYN MONROE OF BURLESQUE.

Still freelancing and with her focus firmly fixed on acting, Marilyn got a part in the United Artists release of a Mary Pickford presentation, *Love Happy*, the last film to star the Marx Brothers. Her role was tiny; she appeared for less than a minute, but she received on screen billing that read: INTRODUCING . . . MARILYN MONROE.

Marilyn and I were to meet in 1954 and know each other for the next eight years, the remainder of her life. Those years hold for me many fond memories of fascinating interludes with her. Once, during some quiet moments alone, I mentioned *Love Happy*, to which Marilyn's entire response consisted of an uproarious laugh at the mere thought of the film's producer Lester Cowan. Something deliciously private no doubt.

But there was little to laugh about during the early months of 1949. Although the William Morris Agency signed her to an American Federation of Radio Artists contract on 2 March, there is no record of any work having come out of this. These were proving hard times: she was not able to secure any film work, modelling jobs were few and far between, and Monroe's already meagre bank balance dwindled to zero. Only one offer loomed: a request to pose for some nude calendar art.

On 29 May 1949 Marilyn Monroe turned up at the studio of photographer Tom Kelley at 736 North Seward Street. Here, in the presence of his wife, Kelley took a series of nude photographs of Monroe, thus entering, inadvertently, the annals of photographic history. The sitting produced some 24 8 x 10 inch colour transparencies of two basic poses: the first a series of full-length profile shots of Marilyn's naked form lounging on a crumpled red-velvet throw; the second of her seated against the same background. During the pose changes, Kelly forgot to change his film plate, resulting in a double exposure.

A smiling MM poses for a publicity portrait for the 1949 release of the Mary Pickford Presentation of the Marx Brothers' last film, United Artists' *Love Happy*, in which her on-screen credit read: 'Introducing . . . Marilyn Monroe.'

A sensuous Marilyn
Monroe poses for a
publicity portrait for
1949's *Love Happy*.

The full-length profile pose was to become the original Marilyn Monroe calender – *A New Wrinkle* – which was released in 1951. Due to its popularity, with Monroe as yet unidentified as the model, it was released again in 1952. When finally it became known that Hollywood's newest sex symbol had posed for the calendar, the second pose shot was released as *Golden Dreams*.

From this source came calendars for 1953, 1954, 1955 and onwards, as well as spin-offs on playing cards, key chain viewers, pens, cigarette lighters, tie clasps, cuff links, serving trays, coasters, drinking glasses, pillowcases, bedsheets and so on. One manufacturer was even so inventive as to construct a rubberized, three-dimensional miniature replica of the *Golden Dreams* pose, which was designed to undulate by turning a crank handle in its base.

One of the more high-profile releases of the *Golden Dreams* pose was its role in launching the *Playboy* magazine empire, with publication in the first issue in December 1953. Having Marilyn Monroe between its covers, that premier edition of *Playboy* was a sell-out. Indeed, had she not been the main attraction inside Hugh Hefner's history-making format, there might never have been a second issue of a magazine called *Playboy*.

Original calendar sales had reached 8 million copies by 1955, with an estimated additional 15 million bootleg copies. Over the past four decades, these Monroe nudes have been published constantly in an inestimable number of magazines and books throughout the world.

Even Kelley's double exposure, a photographic mistake that would normally have gone straight into the rubbish bin, saw publication in America; its appearance in the December 1960 pictorial on Marilyn in *Playboy* is most notable, but it had appeared earlier as the centerfold in the December 1956 issue of *Escapade* magazine.

Of the 21 remaining transparencies, little is known. They were apparently stolen from Tom Kelley's studio years earlier. But those original poses ran and ran. In the early seventies, a full decade after

Above · Golden Dreams Two: The young Marilyn Monroe in a never before seen in the Western world nude by photographer Tom Kelley, photographed on 27 May 1949.

Right A New York store window proudly presents a display of the original *Golden Dreams* calendar.

Above The famous pose, which appeared on all editions of the *Golden Dreams* calendar, including this slightly faded 1956 version.

A dream on location: Virginia MacAllister and
Rusty in front of Photoplay's Dream House

A day that began with smiles. Marilyn Monroe, Donald Buka,
Lon McCallister and Don DeFore at Grand Central Station

While Marilyn and Donald look on, Photoplay's Adele Fletcher presents key to Virginia, who's busy looking for Rusty

the house that dreams built

THE Photoplay Dream House has been built and Virginia MacAllister, the lucky winner, has moved in following a gala, star-studded housewarming.

Early on the morning of the house-warming, a special car attached to the New York Central's crack Empire State Express left New York with a party of very special people to help make the party a success.

Many of them were people you'd know —whether you saw them in Hollywood, your own home town, or in Warrensburg, New York, the site of the Dream House. They were movie stars Don DeFore, Lon McCallister, Donald Buka and Marilyn Monroe. Others included Photoplay's editor Adele Fletcher; Managing editor Ruby Boyd; Cotton Northrup, executive vice-president of the National Retail Lumber Dealers Association (The nation-wide organization (Continued on page 105)

BY JACKIE NEBEN

Did you ever see stars shine in the daytime? Virginia MacAllister did. It was part of the magic that began when she took a chance on a dream

Framed—for his autograph. Don DeFore signs on the dotted line for some of Warrensburg's movie fans

Dirlyte flatware is admired by the two Dons, Marilyn, Virginia

Even Rusty was intrigued by Thor Automagic Clothes Washer Marilyn and Mom showed him

Virginia opened her Lane Cedar Chest to give Marilyn, Donald inside look

Rusty, Donald try To Don and Marilyn, Kleinert show-
Nu-Tone Chimes er curtain suggested nifty sarong

Marilyn and Donald go to work —with Bissell carpet sweeper

Don, Marilyn and Virginia are dazzled by Norge Refrigerator

For store nearest you write direct to manufacturer listed on page 97

PHOTOPLAY FASHIONS

ON THE FASHION GOAL-LINE

A SUIT AND COAT THAT WILL
SCORE ON ANY OCCASION

Slim sorcery: Black stripes accentuate the fitted lines of worsted jacket with gabardine collar and cuffs to match the slim gabardine skirt. By Lou Schneider, in sizes 9-15. It comes in green, wine or copper, about $50.00, at Gimbels, New York, N. Y.

Changeable charm: A dream of a coat in all wool fleece, its full, swinging back can be curbed with a self-belt. Of added interest are the deep, pointed cuffs, double-pointed collar and slashed pockets. By Judy Neil, in winter natural, sizes 10-16, about $35.00, at Bloomingdale's, New York, N. Y.

Handle the new fabrics with loving care—for they're worth investigating. They're at once rough in appearance, soft to the touch and exciting to look at. This autumn, color is as important as fabric, with simplicity the keynote of today's styles. Pockets make their appearance in unexpected fashion. Cuffs are deep, collars intriguingly different. For every-day wear, it's the polished calf look in your shoes, bag and belt. Fashion note this fall is light-colored gloves —and you'll be in the cheering section if you appear in string gloves with your tweeds!

Marilyn Monroe, blonde and lovely foil for the Marx Brothers in United Artists' "Love Happy"

her death, Monroe's *A New Wrinkle* nude was reproduced on posters, puzzles, datebooks and once more on cards and calendars. The photographs are among the most famous images ever to be captured on film.

The 1980s saw three more of the rare Monroe-by-Kelley nudes turn up, all variations of either the *Golden Dream* pose or *A New Wrinkle*. The first, from the *Golden Dream* series, was published in a Japanese book about Monroe; the second and third, both part of *A New Wrinkle*, reached the public domain, the one on a calendar, the other on the American television show *Entertainment Tonight*.

Though there is still such worldwide acclaim and interest in the Marilyn Monroe nudes three decades after her death, in the moral climate of the early fifties these nude photographs could have meant the end of her career as a serious actress. Yet somehow her nakedness came to represent not a moral decline but an erotic uplift – a presage of her original mix of innocence with sensuality. Her timing had been good, and, rather than discredit her, the photographs were to help to turn her into an international sex symbol, the figurehead of a million erotic dreams.

.   .   .

The period following the nude photographic session in Kelley's studio was busy. Her career would go from hot to cold to hot again repeatedly. In June 1949 Monroe went to New York City to plug *Love Happy*. While in the east she took part in a publicity stunt for *Photoplay* magazine with the presentation to winner Virginia MacAllister of her prize in the *Photoplay* Dream House Contest: a home in Warrenberg, New York. The event was covered in *Photoplay*'s November 1949 issue, in which pictures of Marilyn Monroe appear. No stranger to the magazine, she had appeared in it just a month earlier, in a feature on *Photoplay* Fashions.

By late summer Monroe was back in Hollywood, and on 5 August

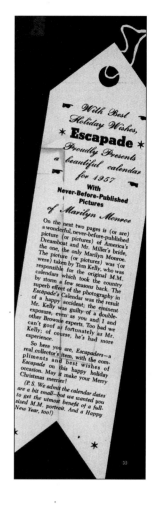

Above and overleaf This double exposure by photographer Tom Kelley miraculously survived, surfacing as a centerfold in the December 1956 issue of *Escapade* magazine.

Opposite
Rare pages featuring Marilyn from 1949 editions of *Photoplay* magazine.

ESCAPADE

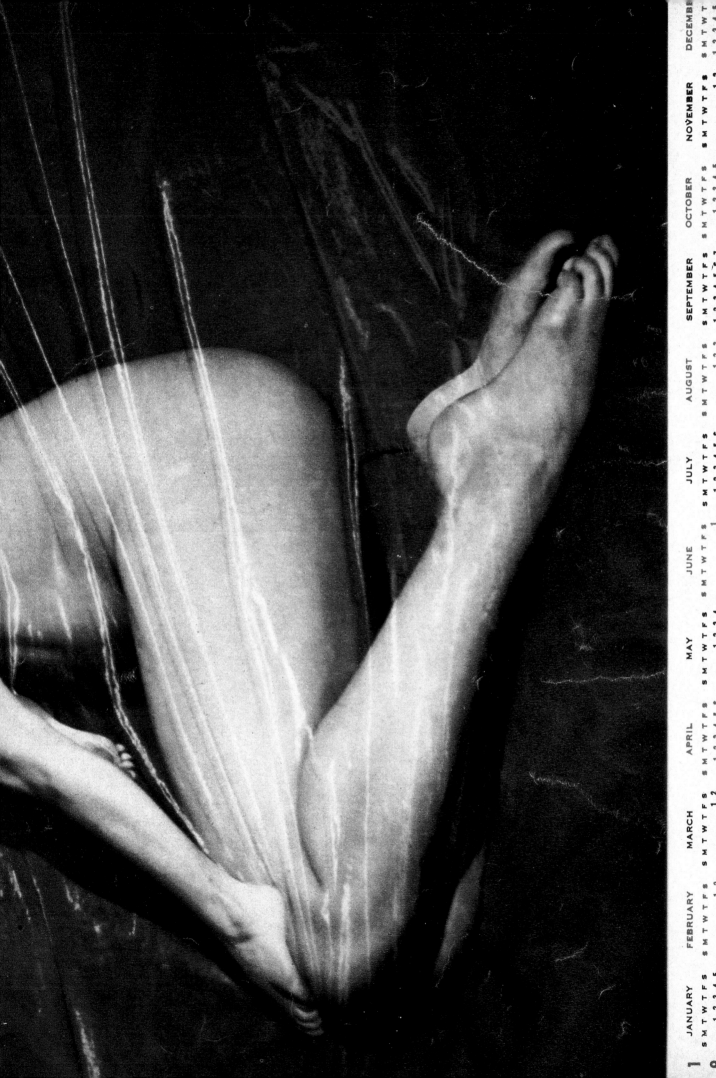

JANUARY
S M T W T F S
1 2 3 4 5
6 7 8 9 10 11 12
13 14 15 16 17 18 19
20 21 22 23 24 25 26
27 28 29 30 31

FEBRUARY
S M T W T F S
1 2
3 4 5 6 7 8 9
10 11 12 13 14 15 16
17 18 19 20 21 22 23
24 25 26 27 28

MARCH
S M T W T F S
1 2
3 4 5 6 7 8 9
10 11 12 13 14 15 16
17 18 19 20 21 22 23
24 25 26 27 28 29 30
31

APRIL
S M T W T F S
1 2 3 4 5 6
7 8 9 10 11 12 13
14 15 16 17 18 19 20
21 22 23 24 25 26 27
28 29 30

MAY
S M T W T F S
1 2 3 4
5 6 7 8 9 10 11
12 13 14 15 16 17 18
19 20 21 22 23 24 25
26 27 28 29 30 31

JUNE
S M T W T F S
1
2 3 4 5 6 7 8
9 10 11 12 13 14 15
16 17 18 19 20 21 22
23 24 25 26 27 28 29
30

JULY
S M T W T F S
1 2 3 4 5 6
7 8 9 10 11 12 13
14 15 16 17 18 19 20
21 22 23 24 25 26 27
28 29 30 31

AUGUST
S M T W T F S
1 2 3
4 5 6 7 8 9 10
11 12 13 14 15 16 17
18 19 20 21 22 23 24
25 26 27 28 29 30 31

SEPTEMBER
S M T W T F S
1 2 3 4 5 6 7
8 9 10 11 12 13 14
15 16 17 18 19 20 21
22 23 24 25 26 27 28
29 30

OCTOBER
S M T W T F S
1 2 3 4 5
6 7 8 9 10 11 12
13 14 15 16 17 18 19
20 21 22 23 24 25 26
27 28 29 30 31

NOVEMBER
S M T W T F S
1 2
3 4 5 6 7 8 9
10 11 12 13 14 15 16
17 18 19 20 21 22 23
24 25 26 27 28 29 30

DECEMBER
S M T W T F S
1 2 3 4 5
8 9 10 11 12
15 16 17 18 19
22 23 24 25 26
29 30 31

SaLe-A581
MARILYN MONROE
AS "CLARA"

CH#1
EXT. FOOTHILLS
ENCAMPMENT-
SC-76-89

8/5/49 · DES HUBERT

1949 she found herself once again on a soundstage at the 20th Century-Fox studios, this time filming a costume test for her small role as Clara in *A Ticket to Tomahawk*. It was a one-shot deal with Fox that took her out of town for a while, for five weeks location shooting in Colorado.

Next, the 10 October issue of *Life* magazine hit the newsstands with photographer Philippe Halsman's photos of the current crop of Hollywood starlets. In an article entitled EIGHT GIRLS TRY OUT MIXED EMOTIONS, she was featured with Suzanne Dalbert, Cathy Downs, Dolores Gardener, Laurette Luez, Lois Maxwell, Jane Nigh and Ricky Soma in a series of photos that depicted their responses to a range of acting situations.

Among the reactions to the piece came this uncanny display of sharp instinct: a note in the Letters column of the 31 October issue of *Life*. A Mrs M. Sakakeeny of Cambridge, Massachusetts, predicted: 'Marilyn Monroe is not only the most beautiful, but the one one who will no doubt make a name for herself in Hollywood.'

Meanwhile Marilyn Monroe was hard at work again, on a Metro-Goldwyn-Mayer production that would subsequently be considered her first important piece of work: the part of Angela Phinlay in director John Huston's *The Asphalt Jungle*.

Then, still as an actress with no studio contract, she moved back to 20th Century-Fox for a small role in the Thor Production of *The Fireball*, which director Tay Garnett had begun filming on 5 January 1950.

Monroe had a minor role in the movie as a girl about town, her scenes mostly taking place ringside at a roller-skating rink, as she watched the roller derby. Her costume in these sequences consisted of a long-sleeved, full-skirted dark dress worn with a light, sleeveless turtle-neck sweater that was pinned down at the collar by a sparkling brooch.

Filming of *The Fireball* was completed in February 1950, when she moved quickly back to MGM for a cameo part in *Right Cross*,

A delighted Marilyn poses for a costume test for 20th Century-Fox's *Ticket to Tomahawk*, the movie that took her to Colorado for five weeks of location filming.

A never before seen
candid portrait taken in
1949, *c.* the filming of
MGM's *The Asphalt
Jungle*.

Shooting for stardom,
Marilyn bewitches the
camera lens in this unseen
image captured in 1949.

the only speaking role that Monroe ever played without an on-screen credit.

Still freelancing, on 2 May 1950 she signed a contract with Fox for a small role in the prestigious production of *All About Eve* that starred Bette Davis. Ironically Marilyn was to play an aspiring actress. In her final scene, which took place in a theatre lobby following a disastrous stage audition, she appeared in the same sweater and skirt outfit that she'd worn in *The Fireball*. Was it part of Fox's vast wardrobe department's stock? Apparently not. For she was to wear that outfit twice more, the final time to some consequence.

Of no immediate consequence for Monroe, June 1950 saw the release of *The Asphalt Jungle*. Monroe could have been forgiven for expecting some kind of major studio interest in her. None was forthcoming.

And so, briefly, she turned her back on the big screen and took up with the rising new medium of television. She accepted commercials work in an advertisement for the Union Oil Company of California, plugging their Royal Triton motor oil with the line: 'Put Royal Triton in Cynthia's [her automobile] little tummy. Cynthia will just love that Royal Triton.' This elusive bit of MM film was televised during the 1950–51 season.

Movie fans who'd seen Marilyn's performance in *The Asphalt Jungle* were able to catch up with her again in the September 1950 issue of *Photoplay*. Here she was the stellar attraction chosen to inaugurate the movie magazine's new series of articles on 'How a Star Is Born', although if Metro-Goldwyn-Mayer's *Home Town Story* had been any measure of Marilyn's future cinematic success, she would not have thrived at all. Even though she again wore that skirt and sweater combo that later bode so well for her.

Distributed by MGM, *Home Town Story* was an institutional film financed by the General Motors Corporation, arriving largely unannounced in the film world, except for a review in the 9 May 1951 edition of *Variety*. With a running time of 61 minutes, it opened in

Marilyn displays that magical combination of sensuality and innocence that caused preview audiences at 1950 screenings of Metro-Goldwyn-Mayer's *The Asphalt Jungle* to enquire, 'Who's the blonde?!'

The girl who would later say, 'I like to feel blonde all over,' protects her fair skin from the sun at New York's Jones Beach in 1949.

'A skeleton in the closet?' Marilyn in a previously unseen publicity photo taken *c.* 1950.

June 1951 at Loew's Metropolitan Theatre in Brooklyn, New York. Monroe was the only member of its cast to be featured in the single advertisement run for it in the local newspapers. *Home Town Story* was not heard of again until 1962, when it surfaced as a re-release in Australia.

The metal cans containing the original 35 mm prints of *Home Town Story* are currently collecting dust in the vaults at Metro-Goldwyn-Mayer, now the Turner Broadcasting Company. This is surely a shame, as they are the missing link for many Marilyn devotees who pride themselves on having viewed every available piece of film footage containing her image.

The fact is that Monroe played a part in *Home Town Story* that was large enough to be commented upon in newspaper reviews at the moment of its first release in 1951, a time that was prior to her real stardom. As part of Monroe's cinematic history, for that reason alone it is well worth viewing.

In 1969, when asked about this missing piece in the Monroe film archive, an MGM executive said that it had never been converted into 16 mm prints for television, 'because we no longer own the rights to it'. But, more than forty years after it played at the Loew's Metropolitan Theatre in Brooklyn, *Home Town Story* finally resurfaced, in a medium that was never encountered by its star: on videotape. On the tabloid television programme *Hard Copy* several of her scenes from the film were shown, the presentation heralded as 'Marilyn's Lost Movie'.

. . .

By the autumn of 1950 Marilyn Monroe had had four years experience in and around the motion picture studios, a mixed time that embraced small cinematic successes as well as two contractual failures. It was a time of waiting, of consolidation. Though at times it must have felt as if her grasp on stardom was fragile. MGM's *The*

Opposite above An informal shot taken on the set of *Home Town Story*, c. 1950–51.

Opposite below left A never before published candid photograph taken circa the filming of *All About Eve*. By the autumn of 1950 Marilyn had had four years experience in and around the motion-picture studios.

Opposite below right Marilyn in a scene from the 1950 20th Century-Fox/Thor Productions' release, *The Fireball*. That's Mickey Rooney, the film's star, on the right. MM wore this same outfit in three other film roles.

Opposite This never before seen candid pin-up pose is around the time of the filming of *The Asphalt Jungle* in 1949.

A wide-eyed Marilyn poses for this studio portrait taken to publicize Metro-Goldwyn-Mayer's 1950 release, *The Asphalt Jungle*, directed by John Huston and considered her first important film role.

Asphalt Jungle should have brought her acclaim. Where was it? In the competitive atmosphere that is Hollywood, a would-be movie star is, after all, only as good as their last film.

In December 1950 20th Century-Fox requested Marilyn do a screen dialogue test for them. The screen-test process was, at that time, the basis upon which executive value judgements were made. A studio would usually make what was called a photographic test, one without sound, of any potentially interesting newcomer. If the test went well, then they would be asked to sign a beginner's contract with the studio. As a matter of course this would contain a clause that gave the studio the option to extend the contract for up to seven years.

Once an individual was signed, then it was only a matter of time before they were given a dialogue test, often lasting as long as 12 minutes screen time. This would involve another actor, giving the studio a chance to see how they performed in a lengthy scene sequence. Obviously these affiliation stages were not set in stone; if an actor were already known to some extent by the studio, then they would clearly bypass the photographic test and possibly film the dialogue test at pre-contract stage. But they were simply variations on a theme that enabled the studio to assign themselves the hottest new properties.

Monroe had already taken a photographic test with 20th Century-Fox in 1946. In the years that followed she had become a familiar face on the movie lot. But, could she survive the examination of a screen test in which she would be the main focus and could make or break a film? Was she made of the stuff of movie stardom? That was the big question in 1950.

The cinematic factories demanded a lot as they turned fantasy into celluloid reality. An actress had – and still has – to embody the essence of fantasy in a reel of illusion, and being young and good-looking helped that process, especially if you were a woman.

Most starlets with Marilyn's same goal had, by her age – 24 – become little more than well-used flesh clinging to the perimeter of an already lost dream. Indeed, many of Marilyn's contemporaries had lost their hold on the Hollywood dream by their mid-twenties. It wasn't too long before her co-stars in 'Eight Girls Try Out Mixed Emotions' were plummeting towards the oblivion of the bottomless cinematic pit.

But Monroe was lucky. She returned again to the studio that had dismissed her three years earlier to make a screen dialogue test. The scene in which Monroe was required to act gave her the part of a gangster's much abused girlfriend – and the opportunity to wear that skirt and sweater outfit once again. It was to become a symbol of luck, though its repeat appearance was most likely a matter of economics. Playing opposite her was the by then well-established actor and star, Richard Conte.

In a determined attempt to find out more about this vital moment in Monroe's career, every effort was made to track down Conte. After following trails that led across the globe, he was finally located not far from where he had taken part in that dialogue test with Marilyn Monroe: Beverly Hills, California.

On 15 January 1975, over the long-distance telephone wires, Richard Conte gave me his recollections of working with Monroe: 'I was under contract to Fox, and I was asked if I would test with a young girl. They asked me if I would test, and I said sure. I think Georgie Jessel was the director.' [Follow-up research was done on George Jessel but it did not come up with any mention of this event in any of his published biographies or press clippings, though Jessel did mention Monroe in other contexts.]

Richard Conte went on to say that he did not recall the source of the material used for the test script – revealed in later research to be a scene from a script entitled *Cold Shoulder* – but he vividly recalled the filming with Marilyn: 'She was quite involved and quite free and concentrated well. She had a natural thing about it; she was quite concentrated.' Then he added, 'The quality of the test was concentrated. I have a print of it.'

A lusty close-up taken around the period of *The Asphalt Jungle*.

Marilyn Monroe is seen here during a portrait sitting in the winter of 1950.

Screen tested and en route to stardom, Marilyn as photographed at 20th Century-Fox, 1950.

And here it is, the very dialogue test that Fox's studio head Darryl F. Zanuck viewed in his executive screening room some forty-four years ago. These are the words that Marilyn Monroe spoke when she made her bid for what subsequently became one of the most spectacular of all motion-picture careers.

My 16mm black-and-white print of Marilyn Monroe's dialogue screen test opens already into the action. It shows a scene of high intensity that takes place after dark in a large living-room. As the sequence begins Richard Conte is seated out of camera range on the edge of a couch. Facing him on camera is an extremely distraught Monroe, who stands in front of a huge fireplace, confronting him in a tone of desperation.

MARILYN MONROE'S SCREEN TEST

FADE IN

MM (*Angry*) Maybe Einstein can figure [it] out. I can't.

RC (*Agitated*) Then what did you come here for?

MM (*Pleadingly*) To tell you you can't stay there. If those gorillas find you here, what happens to them?! [She gestures towards a closed door, indicating other people behind it.] Nothing? They're just gonna leave them alone? What's the matter with you, Benny? You can't take such a chance.

RC (*Rising from the couch*) How did you find out about this?

MM (*Still angry, still in desperation*) Two guys came calling on me, looking for you!

RC (*In a demanding tone*) Who were they?

MM I never saw them before.

RC Well, when did they come?

MM (*In quick, strong tones*) About four o'clock.

[Richard Conte crosses the living-room to the front door. He peers out of the curtains, staring out into the dark night for the men who are pursuing him. MM follows him across the room, and we pick up the scene as Conte turns back towards Monroe and addresses her in great, threatening anger.]

RC   You dumb broad! You stupid little . . .

MM   (*Clearly stunned*) What's the matter?

RC   They followed you here! Or did you bring them with you! I oughta . . .

[He raises his hand to strike her across the face.]

MM   (*Defeated, yet still defiant*) Go ahead! It won't be the first time I've been worked over today (*her voice is trembling*), I'm getting used to it . . .

[She is apparently referring to her earlier run-in with Benny's pursuers. A disgusted Conte gets his jacket and puts it on to leave.]

MM   (*Unsure, still in desperation*) Where're you going?

[Conte doesn't answer; he starts towards the door.]

MM   (*Grabbing his arm, in a plaintive whisper*) Benny . . .

[Conte exits, and there is a lingering, dramatic visual of the now rejected, helpless girl.]

FADE OUT

The director said 'Cut,' and it was over. Marilyn Monroe's dialogue screen test went off to the processing lab. And she waited. She was not alone. Elsewhere a clutch of young movie hopefuls, whose names were destined to become firmly entwined in the Monroe legend, were making their own bids for stardom.

Marilyn Monroe (joined by actor Richard Conte) in her 1950 screen test for 20th Century-Fox, a scene from *Cold Shoulder*.

In England, the girl who'd won a Most Promising Film Actress award in 1947, Diana Dors, was appearing with increasing regularity in the film productions of J. Arthur Rank. (In a review of *The Asphalt Jungle* by a British film critic, Marilyn Monroe was described as a 'Diana Dors lookalike'.) Closer to home, in Austin, Texas, another would-be actress was anticipating her role as a drunkard's wife in the Civic Theatre's production of *Ten Nights In a Barroom*. Her name was Jayne Mansfield. And even closer, in fact in Hollywood itself, a girl named Sheree North walked through the gates of Metro-Goldwyn-Mayer, where she was about to appear fleetingly in *Excuse My Dust*.

Left to right: Patrice Wymore, Marilyn Monroe, Mitzi Gaynor, Leslie Caron, Tony Curtis and John Derek in a 1951 publicity pose.

Working on the seamier side of the film industry were the producers of an early exploitation movie, *A Virgin in Hollywood* (also known as *The Side Streets of Hollywood*). It was to feature Arline Hunter. She would later achieve a vicarious notoriety as the girl who looked enough like Monroe as to pass for her in a number of 1950s stag films, the most notorious of which was *The Apple Knockers and the Coke*.

Universal Pictures got in on the act, too, with another young actress whose career was just beginning: Joan Lucille Olander. She made her debut as an extra in a 1949 John Wayne movie, *Jet Pilot*. By the time of its release by RKO some seven years later, Olander was known to the movie-going public as Universal's Answer to Marilyn Monroe, starlet Mamie Van Doren.

Diana, Jayne, Sheree and Mamie would all reach the height of their movie stardom by the mid-fifties, sustained and enhanced by the star who was to rise higher than all of them: Marilyn Monroe.

Marilyn herself was compared to another great cinematic legend, Jean Harlow. In June 1937 when JEAN HARLOW DIES was the headline in newspapers around the world, Marilyn was 11, then called Norma Jeane Mortenson and still at school. Years later she recalled: 'I remember when Jean Harlow died . . . it was all over the schoolyard.'

A decade and a half later, this comment was made by Erksine

Opposite · All About Eve's
Marilyn Monroe in a
studio portrait taken at
20th Century-Fox in
1950.

Marilyn seen here
in a studio portrait taken
c. the time of her 1950
20th Century-Fox screen
test, which led to her
seven-year contract with
the studio.

Johnson in the New York *World Telegram & Sun*: 'Hollywood took 14 years, three score screen tests and a couple of million dollars to find a successor to Jean Harlow, who melted movie celluloid from 1927 to 1938.' Ironically the article, entitled MARILYN INHERITS HARLOW'S MANTLE, was to appear on 5 August 1952, the date on which, an exact decade later, Marilyn was to die, and the world public would lose yet another of its elusive movie icons.

Somewhere in my archives is a reel of celluloid that contains a quick minute or so of film of Jean Harlow's screen test. The silent black-and-white movie footage shows close-ups of her both full face and in profile. Her personality comes through as utterly exuberant. It was that same special brand of vitality that most closely linked Monroe to Harlow, on screen and off.

A press headline of 5 May 1954 advised: *JEAN HARLOW STORY* SLATED, MARILYN MONROE IS SOUGHT. And, in fact, Monroe did play Harlow once, for a memorable picture published in the 22 December 1958 edition of *Life* magazine.

As Monroe's stature as an actress and sex symbol had become established, there were those whom she had once known who claimed to know her no longer. Jim Dougherty was one such. Monroe's first husband, he was to remark: 'You know, I never knew Marilyn Monroe. I knew Norma Jeane Dougherty. But Marilyn and Norma Jeane were two different people. Norma Jeane was my wife, Marilyn Monroe was a famous movie star. I don't know anything about her life, I never spoke to her. I just didn't know her.'

And so it was at the 1950 première of *The Asphalt Jungle* at Grauman's Chinese Theater in Hollywood. Dougherty was there. He was one of the policemen assigned to the event. A ghost from Marilyn's past, he waited amid the blinding glare of the Kleig lights and popping flashbulbs for the arrival of the stars. Marilyn Monroe did not show up. But the première audience didn't miss her; they were heard to enquire of her appearance on screen: 'Who's the blonde?'

There was another première that year too, for 20th Century-Fox's

The off-screen Monroe as seen here in 1950.

Joe Kirkwood Jr of *Joe Palooka* fame embraces Marilyn during the time they made a TV commercial for Triton Oil.

Appearing in her only television commercial, for Royal Triton Motor Oil, *c.* 1950.

All About Eve on 5 November 1950. Just weeks later Fox was to take the lead in a different way with a positive reaction to Monroe's dialogue screen test. On 10 December 1950 Marilyn Monroe signed a second contract with the studio. It lasted initially for six months, during which she played roles in *As Young as You Feel* and *Love Nest*.

With the start of the new year, January 1951 brought Monroe yet another publicity coup in *Life* magazine, where her elegant colour portrait was captioned Busty Bernhardt. On 29 March she made her only appearance at an Academy Awards ceremony, at which she presented the coveted Oscar statuette to Thomas T. Moulton for Outstanding Achievement in Sound Recording in 20th Century-Fox's *All About Eve*. The event was carried live from coast to coast over the ABC radio network.

Opposite above left
Marilyn takes a back seat to co-stars Jean Peters and David Wayne in this moment 'cut' from the release prints of their 1951 20th Century-Fox film, *As Young As You Feel*. MM had signed a new contract with the studio on 10 December 1950.

Opposite below left
Posing for a portrait to publicize her appearance in Fox's *As Young As You Feel*. This was her first film under her second contract at the studio.

Opposite right A flamboyant publicity pose for *As Young As You Feel*.

CHAPTER THREE

Birth of the Legend

By early summer Monroe's contract was running out. But within hours of its expiration on 10 May, Darryl F. Zanuck had her signature on a third Fox contract, this one to last for a full seven years, all of which would be memorable. A star was on the rise. For many there would never be another like her.

Let's Make It Legal was Monroe's first film under her long-term contract with Fox. It also featured Robert Wagner, then a new, young actor, opposite whom Monroe had recently played in yet another of Fox's screen tests filmed on 14 June 1951. Wagner, who'd been signed up to Fox in 1950 after a dialogue test he'd made with an actress called Pat Knox, later commented on that period of his career.

'I've got 81 screen tests. I made tests with every girl some producer or executive thought would be screen material. It was a terrific experience. I listened and observed as the girls were coached, and it was priceless help.'

Subsequently, at the height of his popularity in the movies, Wagner married former child star, Natalie Wood. Wood had appeared with Monroe in *Scudda Hoo! Scudda Hay!*. And they were later to have a less fortuitous connection, this time in Westwood Memorial Park, their grave sites only yards from each other, with Marilyn's screen test co-star, Richard Conte located between them. Not far from the trio rests Fox studio head, Darryl F. Zanuck.

In those early years of the 1950s, no one would have predicted

Marilyn Monroe plays the role of goddess supreme in this never before published study taken in 1952.

Monroe's premature death. She herself was clearly focussed on life, one that embraced not only the efforts of her work and her acting career but also her personal strivings. Ever the self-educator, she enrolled in a college course.

It must have been odd for Monroe's fellow students to see her one day in class and the next on the cover of *Life* magazine. The issue of 7 April 1952 to be precise. What happened to the young starlet in *All About Eve*, whom director Joseph L. Mankiewicz recalled 'was squeezed into old Betty Grable costumes and used as a dress extra for unimportant bits in some films'?

For one thing the word unimportant was finally dismissed from any juxtaposition with the name Marilyn Monroe. And later Betty Grable herself would reflect: She did an awful lot to boost things up for movies .... There'll never be anyone like her for looks, for attitude, for all of it.'

Monroe went on to film roles in *Clash By Night, We're Not Married, Don't Bother to Knock, Monkey Business* and *O'Henry's Full House*. There were many people who had strong memories of her during 1951–52. Barbara Stanwyck was the star of *Clash By Night*: 'There was a sort of magic about her which we all recognized at once ... she seemed just a carefree kid, and she owned the world.'

And Cary Grant, Marilyn's co-star in *Monkey Business*: 'She seemed very shy, and I remember that when the studio workers would whistle at her, it seemed to embarrass her.'

Fox dress designer Billy Travilla worked – and played – with her too: 'Marilyn and I used to lunch often at the Café de Paris commissary at 20th Century-Fox. I can still see us walking in there, and here's Bette Davis, Tyrone Power, Susan Hayward with their forks frozen halfway to their mouths as they gaped at her. All these stars with their press people and agents and all the background of a studio going on, and it all just stopped dead when Marilyn appeared. It was awesome – and she wasn't even trying.'

A 1951 costume test for 20th Century-Fox's *Love Nest*; her silk-and-satin robe would later turn up on MM in 1952 costume tests for *Gentlemen Prefer Blondes* (see pages 130 and 131).

NEWMAN-A-635
MARILYN MONROE
AS "ROBERTA"
CH #8
INT. APT. DOORWAY
Sc 133

4/12/51   DES-RENIE

Above Arriving at the Oscar ceremonies in Hollywood on 29 March 1951, to present one of the awards. This was her only appearance at an Academy Awards ceremony.

Left Star on the rise, Marilyn dominates the scenery on a Malibu cliff *c.* 1951.

Above A publicity portrait for the 1951 release, *Home Town Story*, distributed by Metro-Goldwyn-Mayer.

Left Marilyn Monroe's second tenure at 20th Century-Fox began with her signature on this contract dated 11 May 1950.

AMERICA'S *MOST EXCITING* PERSONALITY ... MARILYN MONROE. EVERY INCH A WOMAN ... EVERY INCH AN ACTRESS! On movie screens across the country these were the words that were used to announce her arrival on screen in trailers for *Don't Bother to Knock*. And the addendum that followed suggested movie-goers should watch AS THE MOST TALKED ABOUT ACTRESS OF 1952 ... ROCKETS TO STARDOM.

Richard Widmark, her co-star in the film agreed: 'On the set you'd think, Oh, this is impossible; you can't print this. Then you'd see it, and she's got everyone backed off the screen.'

Actress Anne Bancroft made her film debut in the movie: 'On *Don't Bother to Knock* I worked with another newcomer, Marilyn Monroe. It was a remarkable experience! Because it was one of those very rare times in Hollywood when I felt that give-and-take that can only happen when you are working with good actors.

'Marilyn played a baby sitter who has done some very destructive things to this child, and everyone in this hotel had become aware of it. It was the scene where they were bringing her down to the lobby to be held for the police. I was just somebody in the lobby; and I was to walk over to her and react, that's all. There was to be a close-up of her and a close-up of me – you know, to show my reaction.

'Well, I moved towards her, and I saw that girl – of course, she wasn't the big sex symbol she later became, so there was nothing I had to forget or shake off. There was just this scene of one woman seeing another who was helpless and in pain, and she *was* helpless and in pain. It was so real, I responded; I really reacted to her. She moved me so much that tears came into my eyes. Believe me, such moments happened rarely, if ever again, in the early things I was doing out there.'

In 1952 Marilyn Monroe took time off from the studio to undergo an appendectomy. On release from the hospital, she appeared back on the Fox lot to film costume tests for *Niagara*. The tests were shot on 5 May for the film that was the critical turning-point in Monroe's career. Her director, Henry Hathaway, later recalled that 'After I did

Niagara with her, I found her marvellous to work with and terrifically ambitious to do better. And bright.'

The preview publicity trailers thought so too: NIAGARA AND MARILYN MONROE – THE TWO MOST ELECTRIFYING SIGHTS IN THE WORLD!

There was less cause for celebration when on 26 June 1952, Monroe appeared in court in Los Angeles. She was there to speak in her own defence against a pornography ring that was selling mail order nude photographs, which they claimed to be of Monroe herself. Could the aforementioned Arline Hunter have been involved? Whatever, in the end the images were proved bogus, and, in any case, the setback proved a minor irritation in an otherwise smooth running ascent to the dizzying heights of movie stardom.

Clash By Night opened nationwide on 6 August 1952. And the following month, Monroe – then living, according to cheques written at this time, at 2155 Hilldale, Los Angeles, and to be reached at telephone number CR 6 2211 – travelled east to New York City, en route to Atlantic City, New Jersey, and the world première of *Monkey Business*.

While in Atlantic City, Monroe was to play a different kind of role, this time that of Grand Marshal in the Miss America Beauty Pageant Parade along the boardwalk there. And then back to Hollywood to complete filming of *Niagara* as well as guesting on radio's *Edgar Bergen-Charlie McCarthy Show*.

If Monroe's role in *Niagara* was to launch her properly into the Milky Way of Hollywood, then her appearance in *Gentlemen Prefer Blondes* provided the vast momentum to keep her up there. On 12 November 1952 she had stepped on to a soundstage at 20th Century-Fox to film her costume tests for scenes that included her big musical number 'Diamonds Are a Girl's Best Friend'. Originally the song was filmed with Monroe wearing little more than rhinestones to cover up the most intimate parts of her body, while she sang and danced in a burlesque, bump-and-grind fashion, against a black-velvet background.

In the less liberal climate of 1953, reactions to the screening room viewings of the original version were clearly negative, based on the knowledge that parts of the movie would never get past the censors. Monroe's rendition of 'Diamonds Are a Girl's Best Friend' fell into this category, and it was reshot with a covered-up Monroe, encased in a floor-length pink evening gown, which is how she made her appearance in the scene in the release prints.

For the 1953 *Photoplay* Magazine Awards ceremony on 9 February, she had to be sewn into her gold lamé gown. It was an appearance that made some of the other stars there turn green, especially Joan Crawford – although it's not sure whether it was the slinky sensuality of the gown that caused Crawford's jealous anger or the fact that Monroe 'rejected a pass made at her by Joan'.

There was plenty going on for Marilyn Monroe that evening. Her attendance at the *Photoplay* dinner was specific: she was to receive the magazine's New Star Award for her Rapid Rise to Stardom in 1952.

Monroe was fêted wherever she turned. March found her dazzling the crowds at the Hollywood première of Fox's *Call Me Madam*, a film starring Ethel Merman. And 26 June 1953 saw her setting the seal of her success with the imprint of her hands, footprints and signature in the cement outside Grauman's Chinese Theatre. Clearly Marilyn Monroe had arrived.

.   .   .

It is from around this time that we hear of the apocryphal tale of a man who finds himself lost in the wildest, most primitive zones of darkest Africa. Coming upon a tribe in the depths of the jungle, he attempts to communicate with them. Pointing at himself he says, 'Scot . . . American.' And across the tribal chief's face sweeps a wave of relief as he comprehends: 'America . . . Coca Cola, Marilyn Monroe,' he replies.

Marilyn Monroe had become synonymous with all good things

Wearing the gold lamé gown that caused cinema legend Joan Crawford to see red, Marilyn accepts *Photoplay* magazine's 'New Star Award' in Hollywood.

Onlookers gape at Marilyn
out on the town in the
Hollywood of 1951.

Monroe and Andes on location in San Diego, California, for the 1951 filming of their RKO release, *Clash By Night*.

Keith Andes snares co-star Marilyn Monroe in this scene from the 1952 RKO film, *Clash By Night*.

The cover girl of November 1952's *Photoplay*, published to coincide with the British release of *Clash By Night*.

94

American. She attended the publicity merry-go-round of parties and on 13 September 1953 made her television debut on *The Jack Benny Show*, singing 'Bye Bye Baby' to Benny. Norma Jeane was no more! Long live Marilyn!

Her future was to bring marriage to both baseball legend Joe DiMaggio and celebrated playwright Arthur Miller. These two unions would end in divorce for the coming star of such cinema classics as *How to Marry a Millionaire, The Seven Year Itch, Bus Stop, The Prince and the Showgirl, Some Like It Hot* and *The Misfits*.

The inevitable phallic symbol looms skyward behind the budding sex symbol in 1951.

On 5 March 1962, less than five months to the day of her death, Marilyn Monroe attended the Hollywood Foreign Press Association's award ceremonies to receive their Golden Globe statuette as the winner of the category of World Film Favourite Actress. It was an accolade voted for by theatre owners and cinema patrons from all corners of the globe.

Four months later, just weeks before she died, Marilyn Monroe recalled the early years of her career, when she was a young starlet longing for recognition. She remembered the very first time she came across a movie marquee bearing her name: 'I was driving somebody to the airport, and as I came back there was this movie house, and I saw my name in lights. I pulled the car up a distance down the street – it was too much to take up close, you know – all of a sudden. And I said, "God, somebody's made a mistake." But, there it was, in lights.'

During 1952–3, as *Niagara* and *Gentlemen Prefer Blondes* reached the movie theatres of the day, the chemistry crystallized, and the cinema-going public began to flood the fan mail department of 20th Century-Fox with thousands of cards and letters addressed to Marilyn Monroe. It was not long before Monroe became the most popular star not only in Hollywood but also around the world.

I want to say that the people – if I am a star – the people made me a star. No studio, no person – but the people did.

Marilyn strikes a dramatic pose in this full-length glamour portrait taken in 1952.

A rare, never before published candid shot, *c.* 1951. Actress Barbara Stanwyck said of MM: 'There was a sort of magic about her which we all recognized at once . . . she seemed just a carefree kid, and she owned the world.'

A beauteous image taken
around the time of the
1952 film, *Clash By
Night*, an RKO release.

Previous page Marilyn
displays her provocative
figure in this bold yellow
bikini shot taken *c.*
1951–2.

A sultry over-the-shoulder
look in this portrait taken
c. 1952.

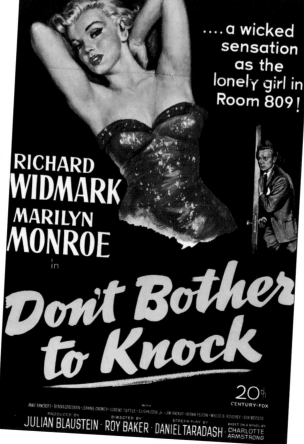

Above A moment cut from the release prints of 20th Century-Fox's *Don't Bother to Knock*. Advance publicity billed her as the most talked about actress of 1952.

Right This 1952 movie poster announces the arrival of a dramatic Marilyn Monroe in the release of *Don't Bother to Knock*. Co-star Richard Widmark said: 'On the set you'd think, Oh, this is impossible; you can't print this. You'd see it, and she's got everyone back off the screen.'

Above With Richard Widmark cheek-to-cheek in this publicity shot for *Don't Bother To Knock*.

Opposite A costume test for *Don't Bother to Knock*. Co-star Anne Bancroft later recalled: 'I really reacted to her. She moved me so much that tears came into my eyes.'

Marilyn Monroe, student, checks the campus map en route to her Backgrounds in Literature classes in February 1952.

Running away with the prize as a beauty contest winner in the 1952 20th Century-Fox release, *We're Not Married*.

A sensational smile for the
camera lens at 20th
Century-Fox in 1952.

Right Displaying her
timeless allure in this 20th
Century-Fox portrait
rescued from the pages of
a 1950s *Photoplay*
magazine.

Above Any description of
the beauty of the Marilyn
Monroe of *Niagara* time
defies mere words.

Above International fame
for Marilyn as exhibited in
Picturegoer at the time of
the British release of
Niagara in May 1953.

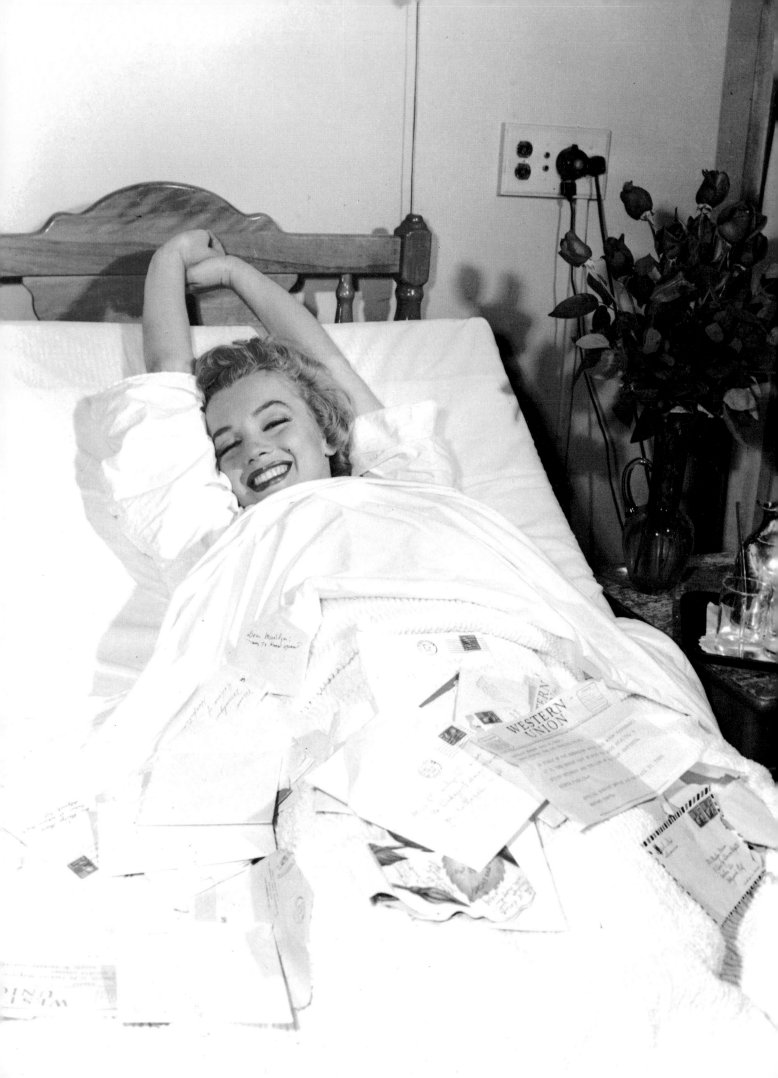

Right A whistle-bait Marilyn poses in New York City in September of 1952, en route to Atlantic City, New Jersey, for the world première of her film *Monkey Business*, a 20th Century-Fox release.

Opposite 6 May 1952: Marilyn receives a flood of get-well messages following her appendectomy.

Above left A rare on-stage appearance at the world première of Fox's *Monkey Business*, in September 1952, at the Stanley Theatre in Atlantic City, New Jersey. Co-star Cary Grant recalled: 'She seemed very shy, and I remember that when the studio workers would whistle at her, it seemed to embarrass her.'

Above right No dummy he, puppet Charlie McCarthy flips his wig for Marilyn in November 1952, during her stint on the Edgar Bergen–Charlie McCarthy radio show.

Opposite A dramatic
Monroe films a costume
test for 20th Century-
Fox's murder mystery,
Niagara, in 1952.

The blonde most
gentlemen were beginning
to prefer is seen here as a
redhead in this portrait
taken in 1952.

Opposite A never before published make-up and hair test for *Niagara*.

Right This sexy shot was captured on the set of *Niagara*.

Opposite Marilyn on the rocks, as captured by the camera lens during the location filming of *Niagara*.

The candid Monroe and canine are seen here at the party in her honour to launch bandleader Ray Anthony's song. 'Marilyn'. Anthony later wed MM cinema shadow, starlet Mamie Van Doren.

Above Actress Marilyn
Monroe and director
Henry Hathaway on the
set of *Niagara* in 1952.
About his star, the director
recalled: 'I found her
marvellous to work with
and terrifically ambitious
to do better. And bright.'

Opposite Hamming it up
with Joseph Cotton in this
shot taken to publicize the
1953 release *Niagara*.

Left An advertisement for
the feature film that
brought about the onset of
MM's genuine movie
stardom, *c.* 1953.

Left Marilyn dons a rose-coloured dress in this costume test shot in 1952 for the 20th Century-Fox film *Niagara*.

Above A costume test for *Niagara*.

Left In a costume test, wearing an outfit that never made it on to the screen in release prints of *Niagara*.

Opposite In this never before seen costume test, Marilyn models a dress in which she was originally set to sing 'Kiss' in *Niagara*. This garment, too, never reached a big screen audience.

An image rescued from an
old movie magazine – a
glamour portrait taken at
20th Century-Fox *c.* 1952.

Right Laughing wildly, in
a studio portrait taken at
20th Century-Fox in
1952.

Above The face of Norma
Jeane lies just beneath the
surface in this close-up
taken in 1953.

Left From the sitting that
would subsequently
inspire Andy Warhol to
immortalize her, Marilyn
is seen in a portrait shot at
20th Century-Fox in
1952.

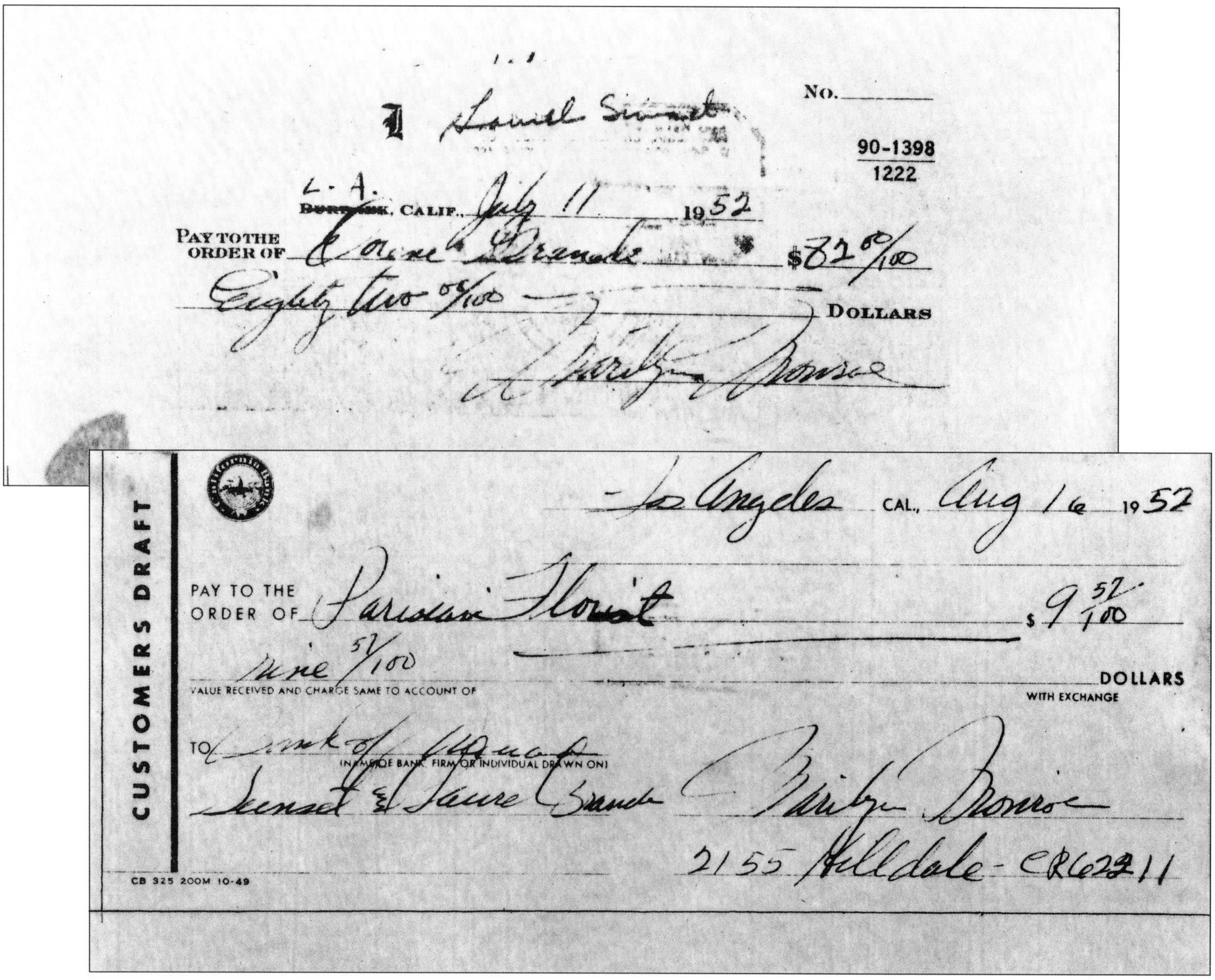

No._____

90-1398
1222

L. A.
BURBANK, CALIF., July 11 1952

PAY TO THE
ORDER OF _____ $82 00/100

Eighty two 00/100 _____ DOLLARS

Marilyn Monroe

CUSTOMERS DRAFT

Los Angeles CAL., Aug 16 1952

PAY TO THE
ORDER OF Parisian Florist

Nine 52/100

VALUE RECEIVED AND CHARGE SAME TO ACCOUNT OF

$9 52/100

DOLLARS
WITH EXCHANGE

TO Bank of America
IN WHOSE BANK, FIRM OR INDIVIDUAL DRAWN ON)

Sunset & Laure Branch

Marilyn Monroe

2155 Hilldale - CR 6 2211

CB 925 200M 10-49

From reel life to real life, some documents from the everyday world of the resident of '2155 Hilldale – CR 6 2211', Los Angeles, California.

In a different kind of appearance, Monroe and her attorney in a Los Angeles courtroom on 26 June 1952, where she was a witness in a case involving nude photos, said to be of her, being sold via the US mails. In the end the images were proved bogus.

Wendell Niles and Marilyn Monroe tape 'Statement In Full' at the NBC studio in Hollywood on 21 August 1952; her radio debut aired on 31 August 1952.

Opposite A moment cut from the release prints of *Niagara*.

Right Monroe's movie lover, actor Richard Allan, chats with the star of *Niagara* on the film's set in 1952.

Above left The cover shot that was used to launch the *Playboy* magazine empire, this image appeared on the first issue, released in December 1953.

Above right Riding on the boardwalk in Atlantic City, New Jersey, Monroe plays the role of Grand Marshal in the September 1952 'Miss America Pageant Parade'.

In these 1952 costume-test shots for 20th Century-Fox's *Gentlemen Prefer Blondes*, Marilyn wears a robe seen earlier in her costume test for *Love Nest* (see page 85).

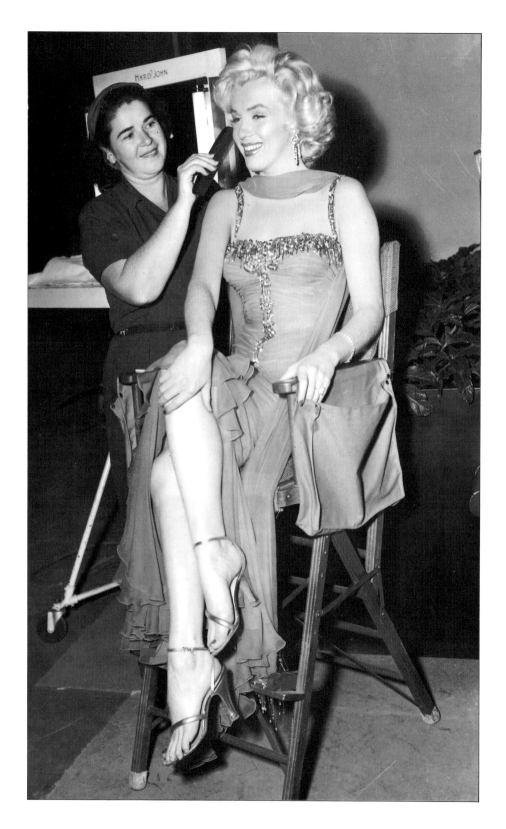

*Opposite · The Face of a
Star* is caught, also, in this
costume test for
Gentlemen Prefer Blondes.
The black slip did not
appear in the final release
prints of film.

Left Marilyn in a relaxed
and candid moment
captured on the set of
Gentlemen Prefer Blondes.

'Gents do prefer blondes'
is the message being
portrayed in this image
taken at 20th Century-Fox
in 1953.

The golden dream girl,
Marilyn Monroe as seen in
this never before
published candid shot
taken in Hollywood, 1953.

Featuring what would
later become a
controversial costume, this
rare test shot is from
*Gentlemen Prefer
Blondes*.

Right Filming her
'Diamonds Are a Girl's
Best Friend' number for
Gentlemen Prefer Blondes.

Previous pages Marilyn
takes a pause during the
January 1953 filming of
her 'Diamonds Are a Girl's
Best Friend' number. This
costume was subsequently
deemed too revealing for
cinema audiences of the
day, and the number was
re-shot featuring the
Monroe figure encased in a
full-length gown.

Opposite and above left
Walking away with the
show at the *Photoplay*
magazine awards night in
Hollywood, 9 February
1953.

Above right Fox's publicity
department announced
that Marilyn had to be
sewn into this gown for the
Photoplay Awards.

Heading for super
stardom, Marilyn is
captured by the camera at
a charity baseball game in
1953. Her name was fast
becoming synonymous
with all good things
American.

Enjoying a repast at the
Photoplay Gold Medal
Awards dinner.

Opposite Photographed in New York City, prior to attending the Atlantic City, New Jersey, world première of her 20th Century-Fox film, *Monkey Business*.

A starry-eyed Marilyn still on the edge of fame in Hollywood, 1951.

Opposite Examining the
Max Reinhardt
manuscripts she
purchased at auction in
December 1952.

In her apartment at 882
North Doheny Drive, Los
Angeles, California, in the
summer of 1953.

Above In pensive mood
reading in her bedroom in
Hollywood in 1951.

Left A serious reader off
screen, Marilyn considers
a passage in *Leaves of
Grass* in this 1951 candid
image.

Opposite Perusing
bookshelves at her
Hollywood apartment
in 1953.

Opposite The coming movie goddess arrives for the première of 20th Century-Fox's *Call Me Madam* in 1953.

Marilyn arrives at the Hollywood première of *Call Me Madam*, wearing a white version of the pink gown used for the re-filming of her 'Diamonds Are a Girl's Best Friend' number in *Gentlemen Prefer Blondes*.

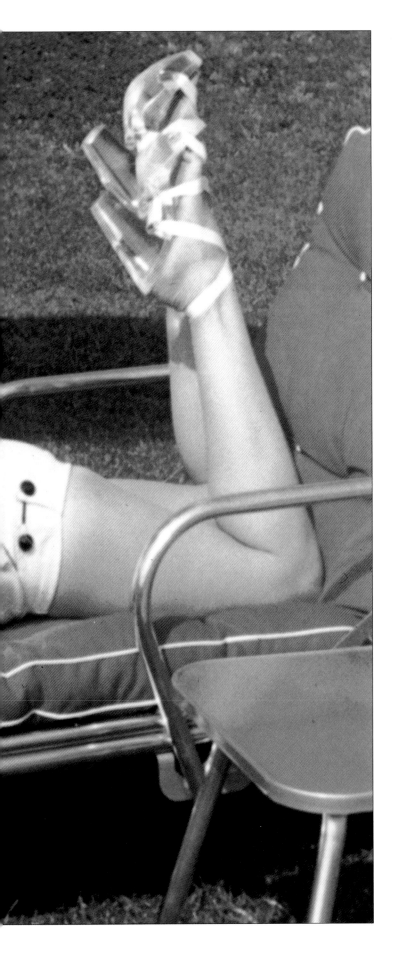

Left Marilyn is seen here in a test shot as she opts to become the spokesperson in an ad campaign for lawn furniture *c.* 1953. When all was said and done, Monroe left both the lounger and the opportunity behind her; the ads never appeared.

Enjoying some champagne in the Hollywood of 1953.

A backseat candid image
taken in 1952.

Marilyn Monroe and Betty
Grable arrive at a party in
Hollywood, 13 May 1953.
About MM, Grable opined:
'She did an awful lot to
boost things up for movies
. . . . There'll never be
anyone like her for looks,
for attitude, for all of it.'

Above With Jane Russell in the opening scene of *Gentlemen Prefer Blondes*, 1953.

Right Marilyn wows the general public from newsstands and magazine racks on this November 1953 cover of *See* magazine.

Above With a display of dazzlingly perfect teeth, Marilyn laughs it up in Hollywood in 1953.

Opposite The ultimate glamour girl bedazzles one and all at a party in the Hollywood of 1953.

Opposite Marilyn Monroe
and Jane Russell are
immortalized in the
cement outside Grauman's
Chinese Theatre in
Hollywood on 26 June 1953.

Above With Jane Russell
filming a scene for
Gentlemen Prefer Blondes.

Right Promoting both her
new film and a hair
product in a 1953 British
magazine.

Opposite A lushly
beautiful Marilyn greets
the camera lens in this
off-screen photo taken
in 1953.

Arriving in satin and
emeralds at a party in
Hollywood in 1953.

Making her official
television debut on *The
Jack Benny Show*, telecast
live on 13 September
1953. She is singing 'Bye
Bye Baby' to Benny.

Glamour girl supreme,
Marilyn Monroe prepares
to attend the première of
her latest film, in
Hollywood, on the night of
4 November 1953.

Opposite An angelic MM
with Jack Benny's
sidekick, Rochester.

The creation of an icon:
Marilyn seen here in a
portrait taken at 20th
Century-Fox some forty-
one years ago.

I want to say that the people – if I am a star – the people made me a star. No studio, no person – but the people did.

And it is those people, and later their children and grandchildren, who have kept Marilyn a star, decades after her passing. In a millennium from now, when that place called Hollywood no longer exists except in a reference work somewhere, the small paragraph that will explain what it was is likely to illustrate the word 'star' with but three examples: Charlie Chaplin, Greta Garbo and Marilyn Monroe.

In this final image, Marilyn Monroe looks to the future in this moving portrait taken at 20th Century-Fox in 1953. The future held not only her untimely demise but also her everlasting stardom.